MW00960259

E G G S

50 Delightful Egg Recipes

For Your Everyday Meals

Celeste Jarabese

Copyright by CONTENT ARCADE PUBLISHING
All rights reserved.

This recipe book is copyright protected and meant for personal use only. No part of this recipe book may be used, paraphrased, reproduced, scanned, distributed, or sold in any printed, or electronic form without permission of the author and the publishing company. Copying pages or any part of this recipe book for any purpose other than own personal use is prohibited and would also mean a violation of copyright law.

DISCLAIMER

Content Arcade Publishing and its authors are joined together in their efforts to create these pages and their publications. Content Arcade Publishing and its authors make no assurance of any kind, stated or implied, with respect to the information provided.

LIMITS OF LIABILITY

Content Arcade Publishing and its authors shall not be held legally responsible in the event of incidental or consequential damages in line with or arising out of, the supplying of the information presented here.

TABLE OF CONTENTS

INTRODUCTION

This book offers many delicious and easy to prepare egg recipes that you can serve for breakfast, lunch, dinner, or snack.

The egg is one of the most versatile and healthy foods that we can have. This book covers traditional egg recipes as well as many interesting new recipes that you can enjoy on any day of the week.

An egg is considered a complete food because it can provide the body with a good amount of protein, fat, vitamins, and minerals. This is also the reason why adding eggs as a part of a healthy diet is recommended by many health professionals.

Now, even with your busy schedule, there is no more reason for you to skip breakfast. Why? It's because egg dishes are very easy to make and would only require a few minutes of your time in the kitchen. You can also add just about any meat, vegetable, or dairy into your egg dishes, which makes them more enjoyable to eat. There is no need to buy special ingredients because, for sure, you already have a few items in your fridge or pantry that could give you a satisfying egg dish in a flash.

Let's get started! Read on and learn how to make that ordinary egg into a remarkable dish!

Tips for Buying, Storing, and Cooking Eggs

The egg is a staple food to many households because it is healthy, economical, easy to prepare, and it only requires a few minutes to cook. Here are a few tips to make sure that you will get that desirable egg dish that you are craving for.

1.   For health-conscious people, an organic egg is the best option.

2.   There are many ways to cook a hard-boiled egg, but the easiest way to do this is by putting the eggs into boiling water and cook for 10 minutes.

3.   When cooking soft-boiled eggs, simmer covered for about 5-7 minutes before serving time to get that runny or barely set egg-yolk.

4.   If you want to achieve fluffy scrambled eggs, add a few tablespoons of milk or mayonnaise then slightly tilt the bowl with eggs while constantly beating to allow some air bubbles to form, but do not overdo it.

5.   When cooking omelettes, allow the egg to cook and fully set at the bottom before adding the filling and gently flipping half of the egg to cover the filling.

6.   Poaching an egg is similar to frying an egg, but instead of oil, you will use water for cooking the egg. Normally, the white part of the egg gets solidified while the yolk remains to be runny.

7.   To test for egg's freshness: Place the uncooked egg in a bowl filled with water. If the egg stays on its side at the bottom, you'll know it is fresh. If the egg floats, then it is no longer fresh and, therefore, not safe to eat.

8.   Using sliced vegetables such as onion and bell pepper is perfect in making egg cups.

9. When buying eggs, look for eggs that are clean and free from cracks.

10. When storing eggs, don't remove them in their original packaging (egg tray) and then place them on the coldest part of the refrigerator. Not on the designed tray that you can find in the door. Properly stored fresh or raw eggs can be kept up to 3-5 weeks, while refrigerated leftover cooked eggs should be consumed within 3 days.

11. If you want to cut down on calories, fat, and cholesterol in your egg dishes, you can substitute half of your egg requirement with egg whites (2 egg whites = 1 egg).

DELIGHTFUL
EGG RECIPES

BAKED EGG IN RED BELL PEPPER CUP

Preparation Time	Total Time	Yield
5 minutes	10 minutes	4 servings

INGREDIENTS

- 4 (60 g) whole eggs
- 4 (35 g) sliced rounds of red bell pepper
- Salt and freshly ground black pepper
- Fresh basil, for garnish
- Cooking oil spray

METHOD

- Preheat your broiler. Take a baking dish or oven-proof pan and grease lightly with oil spray.
- Place 4 slices of red bell pepper into the prepared baking dish.
- Break the egg and fill the center of the bell pepper slices. Spray with some oil and season to taste. Cook in the broiler for 4-5 minutes or to your desired doneness. Remove from heat.
- Transfer to a serving dish. Garnish with fresh basil.
- Serve with and enjoy.

NUTRITIONAL INFORMATION

Energy	Fat	Carbohydrates	Protein	Sodium
117 calories	9.6 g	1.7 g	6.5 g	161 mg

CHEESY POTATO FRITTATA

Preparation Time	Total Time	Yield
10 minutes	20 minutes	6 servings

INGREDIENTS

- 2 tablespoons (30 ml) olive oil
- 1 medium (110 g) white onion, sliced
- 2 new potatoes, thinly sliced (about 200 g each)
- 4 whole eggs (about 60 g each)
- 4 egg whites (about 40 g each)
- 1/3 cup (85 ml) milk
- 1/2 cup (60 g) cheddar cheese, shredded
- Salt and freshly ground black pepper

METHOD

- Preheat your broiler.
- In a large oven-proof pan, heat olive oil over medium flame. Stir-fry the onion for 2-3 minutes or until aromatic.
- Add the potatoes, cover, and cook for 15-20 minutes or until tender but firm.
- Meanwhile, beat together the eggs and milk in a medium bowl. Season to taste. Then pour it into the pan over the potatoes and sprinkle with cheddar cheese. Turn the heat to low, cover with lid, and cook for about 3 minutes.
- Place the pan in the broiler and cook for 5 minutes or until set and the top is golden brown.
- Serve and enjoy.

NUTRITIONAL INFORMATION

Energy	Fat	Carbohydrates	Protein	Sodium
225 calories	11.5 g	19.7 g	11.4 g	238 mg

HERBED TOMATO FRITTATA WITH FETA

Preparation Time	Total Time	Yield
10 minutes	20 minutes	5 servings

INGREDIENTS

- 2 tablespoons (30 ml) olive oil
- 2 (3 g) cloves garlic, minced
- 1 (40 g) shallot, chopped
- 2 (125 g) tomatoes, chopped
- 6 (60 g) whole eggs
- 1/4 cup (60 ml) milk
- 2 tablespoons (30 ml) heavy cream
- 1/2 cup (110 g) feta cheese, crumbled
- 1 tablespoon (3.5 g) dill weed, chopped
- salt and freshly ground black pepper

METHOD

- Preheat and set your oven to 400 F (200 C).
- In a large oven-proof pan, heat olive oil over medium flame. Stir-fry shallot, garlic, and tomatoes for 2-3 minutes or until aromatic and soft.
- Meanwhile, beat together the eggs, milk, and cream in a medium bowl. Season to taste. Pour into the pan over the vegetables. Top with crumbled feta and sprinkle with dill. Turn the heat to low, cover with lid, and cook for about 3 minutes.
- Transfer pan into the oven and bake for 8-10 minutes or until set and golden brown.
- Serve and enjoy.

NUTRITIONAL INFORMATION

Energy	Fat	Carbohydrates	Protein	Sodium
221 calories	17.4 g	6.5 g	11.1 g	280 mg

MINCED CHICKEN AND ONION FRITTATA

Preparation Time	Total Time	Yield
10 minutes	25 minutes	5 servings

INGREDIENTS

- 2 tablespoons (30 ml) olive oil
- 1 medium (110 g) red onion, chopped
- 2 (3 g) cloves garlic, minced
- 8 ounces (250 g) ground chicken
- 6 whole eggs (about 60 g each)
- 1/3 cup (85 ml) milk
- 2 tablespoons (15 g) parmesan cheese, grated
- 1/4 cup (15 g) green onions, chopped
- Salt and freshly ground black pepper

METHOD

- Preheat your broiler.
- In a large oven-proof pan, heat olive oil over medium flame. Stir-fry onion and garlic for 2-3 minutes. Add the minced chicken and cook for 10-12 minutes, stirring occasionally.
- Meanwhile, whisk together the eggs and milk in a bowl. Season to taste. Pour into the pan over the chicken. Sprinkle with parmesan cheese. Turn the heat to low, cover with lid, and cook for 3-5 minutes.
- Transfer pan into the broiler and cook further 5 minutes or until set and golden brown.
- To serve, sprinkle with green onions.
- Enjoy.

NUTRITIONAL INFORMATION

Energy	Fat	Carbohydrates	Protein	Sodium
231 calories	13.8 g	4.0 g	22.6 g	266 mg

PEPPER MUSHROOM AND CHEESE FRITTATA

Preparation Time	Total Time	Yield
10 minutes	30 minutes	5 servings

INGREDIENTS

- 2 tablespoons (30 ml) olive oil
- 1 medium (110 g) white onion, sliced
- 1 medium (120 g) red bell pepper
- 1 ½ cup (225 g) button mushrooms, thinly sliced
- 6 whole eggs (about 60 g each)
- 1/3 cup (85 ml) milk
- 1/4 teaspoon (0.5 g) dried parsley
- 1/4 teaspoon (0.5 g) dried thyme
- 1/4 cup (30 g) cheddar cheese, grated
- Salt and freshly ground black pepper

METHOD

- Preheat and set your oven to 400 F (200 C).
- In a large oven-proof pan, heat olive oil over medium flame. Add the onion and stir-fry for 2-3 minutes or until aromatic. Add the bell pepper and mushrooms; cook, stirring occasionally for 2-3 minutes.
- Meanwhile, beat together the eggs, milk, parsley, and thyme in a medium bowl. Season with salt and pepper. Then pour the egg mixture over the vegetables in the pan. Sprinkle with cheddar cheese. Turn the heat to low, cover with lid, and cook for 3-4 minutes.
- Place the pan in the oven and bake for 10 minutes or until set and golden brown.
- Serve and enjoy.

NUTRITIONAL INFORMATION

Energy	Fat	Carbohydrates	Protein	Sodium
186 calories	13.9 g	5.9 g	10.6 g	246 mg

POTATO ONION AND PEA FRITTATA

Preparation Time	Total Time	Yield
10 minutes	30 minutes	5 servings

INGREDIENTS

- 2 tablespoons (30 g) butter
- 2 potatoes, thinly sliced (about 150 g each)
- 1/2 cup (90 g) frozen green peas, thawed
- 1/3 cup (55 g) shallots, chopped
- 1 teaspoon (3 g) garlic, minced
- 5 whole eggs (about 60 g each)
- 3 egg whites (about 40 g each)
- 3 tablespoons (45 ml) half and half cream
- 2 tablespoons (7 g) fresh parsley, chopped
- Chopped green onion, for garnish
- Salt and freshly ground black pepper

METHOD

- Preheat your broiler.
- In a large oven-proof pan, melt butter over medium flame. Add the shallots and garlic, stir-fry for 2-3 minutes or until aromatic.
- Add the potatoes and green peas. Cover with lid and cook for about 15-20 minutes, or until potatoes are tender, stirring occasionally.
- Meanwhile, beat the eggs and cream in a medium bowl. Season to taste. Pour the egg mixture over vegetables and sprinkle with parsley. Turn the heat to low, cover with lid, and cook for 3-5 minutes.
- Place the pan in the broiler and cook for another 5

minutes or until set and golden brown.
- Sprinkle with chopped green onion before serving.
- Enjoy.

NUTRITIONAL INFORMATION

Energy	Fat	Carbohydrates	Protein	Sodium
213 calories	10.1 g	19.5 g	11.7 g	255 mg

CHEESY VEGETABLE FRITTATA

Preparation Time	Total Time	Yield
10 minutes	25 minutes	5 servings

INGREDIENTS

- 2 tablespoons (30 ml) olive oil
- 1 medium (110 g) onion, chopped
- 1 teaspoon (3 g) garlic, minced
- 1 medium (230 g) fennel bulb, shredded
- 1 cup (150 g) frozen mixed vegetables, thawed
- 4 whole eggs (about 60 g each)
- 4 egg whites (about 40 g each)
- 1/3 cup (85 ml) milk
- 1/4 cup (30 g) mozzarella cheese, grated
- 2 tablespoons (15 g) cheddar cheese, grated
- 2 tablespoons (15 g) parmesan, finely grated
- Freshly ground black pepper

METHOD

- Preheat and set your oven to 400 F (200 C).
- In a small bowl, combine the mozzarella cheese, cheddar cheese, and parmesan cheese. Mix well then set aside.
- In a large oven-proof pan, heat oil over medium flame. Stir-fry onion and garlic for 2-3 minutes or until aromatic.
- Add the fennel and mixed vegetables; cover and cook for 5 minutes.
- Meanwhile, whisk together the eggs and milk in a

medium bowl. Season to taste. Pour the egg mixture over vegetables. Turn the heat to low, cover with lid, and cook for 3-5 minutes.

- Sprinkle with cheese mixture and then transfer the pan into the oven and bake for 10 minutes or until set and golden brown.
- Serve and enjoy.

NUTRITIONAL INFORMATION

Energy	Fat	Carbohydrates	Protein	Sodium
198 calories	11.7 g	12.1 g	12.1 g	289 mg

POTATO FENNEL AND TOMATO FRITTATA

Preparation Time	Total Time	Yield
10 minutes	30 minutes	6 servings

INGREDIENTS

- 2 tablespoons (30 g) butter, unsalted
- 2 potatoes (about 150 g each), sliced thinly
- 1/2 medium (115 g) fennel bulb, shredded
- 3/4 cup (115 g) cherry tomatoes, halved
- 1/3 cup (55 g) shallots, sliced
- 1 teaspoon (3 g) garlic, minced
- 5 whole eggs (about 60 g each)
- 3 egg whites (about 40 g each)
- 1/3 cup (85 ml) milk
- 1/4 cup (30 g) cheddar cheese, grated
- 2 tablespoons (7 g) fresh parsley, chopped
- Salt and freshly ground black pepper

METHOD

- Preheat your broiler.
- In a large non-stick pan, melt butter over medium-heat. Add the shallots and garlic, stir-fry for 2-3 minutes or until aromatic.
- Add potatoes, fennel, and cherry tomatoes. Cover and cook for 15 minutes or until potatoes are tender, stirring occasionally.
- Meanwhile, whisk together the eggs and milk in a medium bowl. Season to taste and set aside.
- Transfer the cooked vegetables into a baking dish then pour the egg mixture, and sprinkle with cheese and

parsley. Cook in the broiler for another 5-7 minutes or until set and golden brown.

- Serve and enjoy.

NUTRITIONAL INFORMATION

Energy	Fat	Carbohydrates	Protein	Sodium
198 calories	10.1 g	17.0 g	10.7 g	252 mg

SPINACH MUSHROOM AND HERB FRITTATA

Preparation Time	Total Time	Yield
10 minutes	25 minutes	5 servings

INGREDIENTS

- 2 tablespoons (30 ml) olive oil
- 1 medium (110 g) onion, sliced
- 1 teaspoon (3 g) garlic, minced
- 8 ounces (250 g) baby spinach
- 1 cup (150 g) button mushroom, sliced
- 6 whole eggs (about 60 g each)
- 1/3 cup (85 ml) milk
- 1 teaspoon (2 g) paprika
- 1/4 teaspoon (0.5 g) dried thyme
- 1/4 teaspoon (0.5 g) dried rosemary
- Salt and freshly ground black pepper

METHOD

- Preheat and set your oven to 400 F (200 C).
- In a large oven-proof pan, heat olive oil over medium-heat. Stir-fry onion and garlic for 2-3 minutes or until fragrant.
- Add the spinach and mushrooms. Cover and cook for 3 minutes or until spinach is wilted, stirring occasionally.
- Meanwhile, whisk together the eggs and milk in a medium bowl. Season to taste. Pour the egg mixture over vegetables in the pan, and then sprinkle with herbs. Turn the heat to low, cover with lid, and cook for 3-5 minutes.

- Transfer the pan into the oven and bake for 10 minutes or until set and golden brown.
- Serve and enjoy.

NUTRITIONAL INFORMATION

Energy	Fat	Carbohydrates	Protein	Sodium
169 calories	12.2 g	6.3 g	10.4 g	247 mg

PEPPER TOMATO AND CHEESE FRITTATA

Preparation Time	Total Time	Yield
10 minutes	25 minutes	6 servings

INGREDIENTS

- 2 tablespoons (30 ml) olive oil
- 2 shallots (about 40 g each), chopped
- 1 teaspoon (3 g) garlic, minced
- 1/2 medium (60 g) yellow bell pepper, deseeded and diced
- 1/2 medium (60 g) red bell pepper, deseeded and diced
- 1/2 cup (75 g) grape tomatoes, diced
- 5 whole eggs (about 60 g each)
- 4 egg whites (about 40 g each)
- 3 tablespoons (45 ml) half and half cream
- 1/3 cup (40 g) cheddar cheese, grated
- Salt and freshly ground black pepper

METHOD

- Preheat your broiler.
- In a large oven-proof pan, heat olive oil over medium flame. Add the shallots and garlic, stir-fry for 2-3 minutes or until aromatic.
- Add the peppers and tomatoes; cook for 3-5 minutes, stirring occasionally.
- Meanwhile, whisk together the eggs and cream in a medium bowl. Season to taste. Pour egg mixture over the peppers and tomatoes then sprinkle with cheese. Turn the heat to low, cover with lid, and cook for 2-3

minutes.
- Transfer the pan into the broiler and cook further 5 minutes or until set and golden brown.
- Serve and enjoy.

NUTRITIONAL INFORMATION

Energy	Fat	Carbohydrates	Protein	Sodium
146 calories	10.5 g	4.5 g	9.2 g	117 mg

TOMATO AND MUSHROOM FRITTATA WITH PARMESAN

Preparation Time	Total Time	Yield
10 minutes	25 minutes	5 servings

INGREDIENTS

- 2 tablespoons (30 ml) olive oil
- 1 medium (110 g) onion, chopped
- 2 (3 g) cloves garlic, minced
- 2 medium tomatoes (about 125 g each), chopped
- 1 cup (150 g) button mushrooms, sliced
- 6 whole eggs (about 60 g each)
- 1/4 cup (60 ml) milk
- 3 Tbsp. (20 g) parmesan cheese, grated
- 1/4 teaspoon (0.5 g) dried oregano
- 1/4 teaspoon (0.5 g) dried sage
- Salt and freshly ground black pepper

METHOD

- Preheat and set your oven to 400 F (200 C).
- In a large oven-proof pan, heat olive oil over medium flame. Stir-fry onion and garlic for 2-3 minutes or until aromatic.
- Add the tomatoes and mushrooms; cook for 3-5 minutes, stirring occasionally.
- Meanwhile, whisk together the eggs, milk, and parmesan cheese in a medium bowl. Season to taste then pour over the vegetables in the pan. Sprinkle with

dried oregano and sage. Turn the heat to low, cover with lid, and cook for 2-3 minutes.
- Transfer pan into the oven and bake for 10 minutes or until set and golden brown.
- Serve and enjoy.

NUTRITIONAL INFORMATION

Energy	Fat	Carbohydrates	Protein	Sodium
176 calories	12.7 g	6.5 g	10.5 g	241 mg

HERBED TUNA AND SPINACH FRITTATA

Preparation Time	Total Time	Yield
10 minutes	25 minutes	5 servings

INGREDIENTS

- 2 tablespoons (30 ml) olive oil
- 1 medium (110 g) red onion, chopped
- 2 (3 g) cloves garlic, minced
- 6 ounces (185 g) canned tuna in water, flaked
- 2 cups (60 g) baby spinach
- 4 whole eggs (about 60 g each)
- 4 egg whites (about 40 g each)
- 1/3 cup (85 ml) milk
- 2 tablespoons (7 g) fresh basil, chopped
- 2 tablespoons (7 g) fresh parsley, chopped
- Salt and freshly ground black pepper

METHOD

- Preheat your broiler.
- In a large oven-proof pan, heat olive oil over medium flame. Add the onion and garlic, stir-fry for 2-3 minutes or until fragrant.
- Add tuna, spinach, basil, and parsley. Cook for 3-5 minutes, stirring occasionally.
- Meanwhile, whisk together the eggs and milk in a medium bowl. Season to taste then pour over the tuna and spinach in the pan. Turn the heat to low, cover with lid, and cook for 2-3 minutes.
- Place the pan in the broiler and cook for another 5 minutes or until set and golden brown.

- Serve and enjoy.

NUTRITIONAL INFORMATION

Energy	Fat	Carbohydrates	Protein	Sodium
197 calories	12.0 g	4.2 g	18.3 g	246 mg

ZUCCHINI FRITTATA WITH DILL

Preparation Time	Total Time	Yield
10 minutes	25 minutes	5 servings

INGREDIENTS

- 2 tablespoons (30 ml) olive oil
- 1 medium (110 g) red onion, chopped
- 1 teaspoon (3 g) garlic, minced
- 1 medium (200 g) zucchini, thinly sliced
- 1 tablespoon (3.5 g) fresh dill, chopped
- 5 whole eggs (about 60 g each)
- 3 egg whites (about 40 g each)
- 1/4 cup (85 ml) sour cream
- 1/3 cup (40 g) cheddar cheese, grated
- Salt and freshly ground black pepper

METHOD

- Preheat your broiler.
- In a large oven-proof pan, heat olive oil over medium flame. Stir-fry onion and garlic for 2-3 minutes or until fragrant.
- Add the zucchini slices and dill weed. Cover and cook for 7 minutes or until tender, stirring occasionally.
- Meanwhile, whisk together the eggs and sour cream in a medium bowl. Season to taste then pour mixture over the zucchini. Turn the heat to low, cover, and cook for 3-5 minutes. Sprinkle with cheese.
- Place the pan in the broiler and cook for another 5 minutes or until set and golden brown.
- Serve and enjoy.

NUTRITIONAL INFORMATION

Energy	Fat	Carbohydrates	Protein	Sodium
189 calories	13.5 g	5.3 g	12.4 g	273 mg

MINI FRITTATAS WITH COTTAGE CHEESE AND CHIVES

Preparation Time	Total Time	Yield
10 minutes	25 minutes	8 servings

INGREDIENTS

- 2 tablespoons (30 g) unsalted butter
- 1/2 cup (60 g) chopped chives
- 1 cup (220 g) cottage cheese
- 6 eggs (about 60 g each)
- 4 egg whites (about 40 g each)
- 1/2 cup (125 ml) skim milk
- Salt and freshly ground black pepper
- Cooking oil spray

METHOD

- Preheat and set your oven to 400 F (200 C). Lightly grease a muffin pan with cooking oil spray.
- Melt butter in a skillet over medium heat, stir-fry half of the chives for 1 minute. Set aside.
- Beat the eggs in a medium bowl. Stir in the milk, sautéed chives, and cottage cheese. Mix well and season to taste.
- Pour mixture into the prepared muffin pan. Place inside the oven and cook for about 15 minutes or until golden and puffy.
- Transfer to a serving dish and sprinkle with remaining chives.
- Serve and enjoy.

NUTRITIONAL INFORMATION

Energy	Fat	Carbohydrates	Protein	Sodium
111 calories	6.7 g	5.3 g	12.4 g	202 mg

SPINACH TOMATO AND CHEESE FRITTATA

Preparation Time	Total Time	Yield
5 minutes	20 minutes	4 servings

INGREDIENTS

- 2 tablespoons (30 ml) olive oil
- 1 (40 g) shallot, chopped
- 1 teaspoon (3 g) garlic, minced
- 1/4 teaspoon (0.5 g) dried thyme
- 2 cups (60 g) baby spinach
- 1 cup (150 g) cherry tomatoes
- 6 whole eggs (about 60 g each)
- 1/3 cup (85 ml) low-fat milk
- 1/4 cup (30 g) mozzarella cheese, grated
- Salt and freshly ground black pepper

METHOD

- Preheat and set your oven to 400 F (200 C).
- Heat the oil in an oven-proof pan or skillet over medium flame. Sauté the shallot and garlic for 2-3 minutes or until fragrant.
- Add the spinach and cook for 2 minutes or until wilted.
- Whisk together the eggs and milk in a mixing bowl. Season to taste.
- Pour the egg mixture over sautéed spinach, and cook for about 3 minutes or until the edges start to brown. Sprinkle with mozzarella and then top with cherry tomatoes.
- Place the pan inside the oven and cook for 10 minutes more or until the center is set.

- Serve and enjoy.

NUTRITIONAL INFORMATION

Energy	Fat	Carbohydrates	Protein	Sodium
206 calories	15.2 g	7.0 g	11.9 g	247 mg

CREAMY SCRAMBLED EGGS WITH TOMATOES

Preparation Time	Total Time	Yield
5 minutes	15 minutes	4 servings

INGREDIENTS

- 4 whole eggs (about 60 g each)
- 3 egg whites (about 40 g each)
- 2 tablespoons (30 ml) milk
- 2 tablespoons (30 g) mayonnaise
- 2 tablespoons (30 ml) olive oil
- 1 medium (110 g) onion, chopped
- 1 teaspoon (3 g) garlic, minced
- 1 cup (150 g) cherry tomatoes, quartered
- 1 teaspoon (2 g) paprika
- Salt and freshly ground black pepper

METHOD

- Whisk the eggs then stir in milk and mayonnaise in a medium bowl.
- Heat the oil in a large non-stick skillet or pan over medium flame. Stir-fry onion and garlic for 2-3 minutes.
- Add the cherry tomatoes and paprika; cook for 3-4 minutes, stirring occasionally.
- Pour the egg mixture into the skillet; cook, stirring often for 2-3 minutes or to desired doneness. Season to taste.
- Transfer to a serving dish.
- Serve and enjoy.

NUTRITIONAL INFORMATION

Energy	Fat	Carbohydrates	Protein	Sodium
198 calories	14.8 g	7.5 g	10.1 g	254 mg

SCRAMBLED EGGS WITH CHICKEN AND HERB

Preparation Time	Total Time	Yield
5 minutes	15 minutes	5 servings

INGREDIENTS

- 6 whole eggs (about 60 g each)
- 4 egg whites (about 40 g each)
- 1/3 cup (85 ml) milk
- 2 tablespoons (30 ml) olive oil
- 1 teaspoon (3 g) garlic, minced
- 8 oz. (250 g) chicken breast fillet, minced
- 1/2 teaspoon (1 g) ground coriander seeds
- 1/4 teaspoon (0.5 g) dried rosemary
- 1/4 teaspoon (0.5 g) dried thyme
- Salt and freshly ground black pepper

METHOD

- Whisk together the eggs and milk in a mixing bowl then set aside.
- Heat oil in a large non-stick pan or skillet over medium-high flame. Stir-fry garlic for 2-3 minutes.
- Add the minced chicken, coriander, rosemary, and thyme; cook for 7-10 minutes or until browned and cooked through, stirring occasionally.
- Pour the egg-milk mixture into the pan; cook, stirring often for 2-3 minutes or to desired doneness. Season to taste.
- Transfer to a serving dish.
- Serve and enjoy.

NUTRITIONAL INFORMATION

Energy	Fat	Carbohydrates	Protein	Sodium
244 calories	15.4 g	1.7 g	24.2 g	274 mg

SCRAMBLED EGGS WITH FETA AND PARSLEY

Preparation Time	Total Time	Yield
5 minutes	15 minutes	4 servings

INGREDIENTS

- 4 whole eggs (about 60 g each)
- 3 egg whites (about 40 g each)
- 1/4 cup (60 ml) milk
- 2 tablespoons (30 g) butter
- 1 (40 g) shallot, chopped
- 1 (3 g) clove garlic, minced
- 1/2 cup (110 g) feta cheese
- 2 tablespoons (7 g) fresh parsley, chopped
- Salt and freshly ground black pepper

METHOD

- Whisk together the eggs, milk, and feta cheese in a medium bowl.
- Melt butter in a large non-stick pan or skillet over medium flame. Add the shallot and garlic, stir-fry for 2-3 minutes.
- Pour the egg mixture into the pan then sprinkle with parsley; cook, stirring often for 2-3 minutes or to desired doneness. Season to taste.
- Serve and enjoy.

NUTRITIONAL INFORMATION

Energy	Fat	Carbohydrates	Protein	Sodium
181 calories	11.7 g	5.3 g	13.8 g	205 mg

SCRAMBLED EGGS WITH MUSHROOM AND CHEDDAR

Preparation Time	Total Time	Yield
5 minutes	15 minutes	4 servings

INGREDIENTS

- 4 whole eggs (about 60 g)
- 3 egg whites (about (40 g)
- 2 tablespoons (30 g) mayonnaise
- 2 tablespoons (20 ml) olive oil
- 1 teaspoon (3 g) garlic, minced
- 1 cup (150 g) button mushrooms, sliced
- 1/2 teaspoon (1 g) ground cumin
- 1/4 teaspoon (0.5 g) dried sage
- 1/4 cup (30 g) cheddar cheese, grated
- Salt and freshly ground black pepper

METHOD

- Whisk together the eggs and mayonnaise in a medium bowl. Set aside.
- Heat oil in a large non-stick pan or skillet over medium flame. Stir-fry garlic for 2-3 minutes.
- Add the button mushrooms, cumin, and sage; cook for 2-3 minutes, stirring frequently.
- Pour the egg mixture into the pan, and then sprinkle with cheese; cook, stirring often for 2-3 minutes or to desired doneness. Season to taste.
- Transfer to a serving dish.
- Serve and enjoy.

NUTRITIONAL INFORMATION

Energy	Fat	Carbohydrates	Protein	Sodium
185 calories	13.4 g	3.9 g	12.6 g	201 mg

SCRAMBLED EGGS WITH ONION AND TOMATO

Preparation Time	Total Time	Yield
5 minutes	15 minutes	4 servings

INGREDIENTS

- 5 (60 g) whole eggs
- 1/4 cup (60 ml) milk
- 2 tablespoons (30 ml) olive oil
- 2 (110 g) white onion, chopped
- 2 (3 g) cloves garlic, minced
- 2 (125 g) tomatoes, chopped
- 2 tablespoons (7 g) fresh parsley
- Salt and freshly ground black pepper

METHOD

- Whisk the eggs and stir in milk in a medium bowl.
- Heat oil in a large non-stick pan or skillet over medium-high flame. Stir-fry onion and garlic until aromatic, about 2-3 minutes.
- Add the tomatoes; cook for 2-3 minutes, stirring occasionally.
- Pour the egg-milk mixture into the pan. Add the parsley; cook, stirring constantly for 2-3 minutes or to desired doneness. Season to taste.
- Serve and enjoy.

NUTRITIONAL INFORMATION

Energy	Fat	Carbohydrates	Protein	Sodium
186 calories	13.7 g	7.7 g	9.5 g	248 mg

FLUFFY SCRAMBLED EGGS WITH PARMESAN

Preparation Time	Total Time	Yield
5 minutes	15 minutes	5 servings

INGREDIENTS

- 4 (60 g) whole eggs
- 4 (40 g) egg whites
- 2 tablespoons (30 g) mayonnaise
- 2 tablespoons (30 ml) milk
- 2 tablespoons (30 ml) olive oil
- 1/3 cup (55 g) shallots, chopped
- 1 teaspoon (3 g) garlic, minced
- 1/4 cup (30 g) parmesan cheese, grated
- 2 tablespoons (7 g) fresh parsley, chopped
- Salt and freshly ground black pepper

METHOD

- Beat together the eggs, mayonnaise, and milk in a medium bowl.
- Heat oil in a large non-stick pan or skillet over medium flame. Add the shallots and garlic, stir-fry for 2-3 minutes.
- Pour the egg mixture into the pan, and then sprinkle with parmesan and chopped parsley. Cook, stirring constantly for 2-3 minutes or to your desired doneness. Season to taste.
- Transfer to a serving dish.
- Serve and enjoy.

NUTRITIONAL INFORMATION

Energy	Fat	Carbohydrates	Protein	Sodium
186 calories	13.7 g	3.5 g	12.5 g	253 mg

SCRAMBLED EGGS WITH PEPPER TOMATO AND GARLIC

Preparation Time	Total Time	Yield
5 minutes	15 minutes	4 servings

INGREDIENTS

- 4 whole eggs (about 60 g each)
- 2 egg whites (about 40 g each)
- 3 tablespoons (45 ml) milk
- 2 tablespoons (30 ml) olive oil
- 1 teaspoon (3 g) garlic, minced
- 2 medium tomatoes (about 125 g each), chopped
- 1/2 medium (60 g) red bell pepper, deseeded and chopped
- 1/2 medium (60 g) green bell pepper, deseeded and chopped
- 1 teaspoon (2 g) cayenne pepper powder
- 1/4 teaspoon (0.5 g) dried basil
- Salt and freshly ground black pepper

METHOD

- Whisk the together the eggs and milk in a medium bowl.
- Heat oil in a large non-stick pan or skillet over medium-high flame. Stir-fry garlic for 2-3 minutes.
- Add the tomatoes, peppers, and dried basil; cook for 2-3 minutes, stirring occasionally.
- Pour the egg mixture into the pan; cook, stirring often

for 2-3 minutes or to desired doneness. Season to taste.
- Transfer to a serving dish.
- Serve and enjoy.

NUTRITIONAL INFORMATION

Energy	Fat	Carbohydrates	Protein	Sodium
169 calories	12.4 g	6.1 g	9.3 g	242 mg

SCRAMBLED EGGS WITH TUNA AND ALFALFA

Preparation Time	Total Time	Yield
5 minutes	15 minutes	4 servings

INGREDIENTS

- 4 whole eggs (about 60 g each)
- 3 egg whites (about 40 g each)
- 3 tablespoons (45 ml) half and half cream
- 2 tablespoons (30 ml) olive oil
- 1 medium (110 g) onion, chopped
- 1 teaspoon (3 g) garlic, minced
- 6 ounces (185 g) canned tuna flakes in water, drained
- 1/4 teaspoon (0.5 g) dried dill
- 1/4 teaspoon (0.5 g) dried thyme
- 1 cup (30 g) alfalfa sprouts
- Salt and freshly ground black pepper

METHOD

- Whisk together the eggs and cream in a medium bowl.
- Heat oil in a large non-stick pan or skillet over medium flame. Stir-fry onion and garlic until aromatic, about 2-3 minutes.
- Add the tuna flakes, dill, and thyme; cook for 2-3 minutes, stirring occasionally.
- Pour the beaten egg mixture into the pan; cook, stirring often for 2-3 minutes or to desired doneness. Season to taste.
- Transfer to a serving dish and top with alfalfa sprouts.

- Serve and enjoy.

NUTRITIONAL INFORMATION

Energy	Fat	Carbohydrates	Protein	Sodium
243 calories	15.7 g	4.2 g	21.3 g	269 mg

SCRAMBLED EGGS WITH TOMATO AND PAPRIKA

Preparation Time	Total Time	Yield
5 minutes	15 minutes	4 servings

INGREDIENTS

- 4 whole eggs (about 60 g each)
- 2 egg whites (about 40 g each)
- 3 tablespoons (45 g) sour cream
- 2 tablespoons (30 ml) olive oil
- 1/3 cup (55 g) shallots, chopped
- 1 teaspoon (3 g) garlic, minced
- 2 medium tomatoes (about 125 g each), chopped
- 2 teaspoons (4 g) sweet paprika, divided
- Salt and freshly ground black pepper

METHOD

- In a medium bowl, whisk together the eggs and sour cream.
- Heat oil in a large non-stick pan or skillet over medium flame. Add the shallots and garlic, stir-fry for 2-3 minutes or until aromatic.
- Add the tomatoes and 1 teaspoon paprika; cook for 2-3 minutes, stirring occasionally.
- Pour the egg mixture into the pan; cook, stirring often for 2-3 minutes or to desired doneness. Season to taste.
- Transfer to a serving dish and sprinkle with remaining 1 teaspoon of paprika.
- Serve and enjoy.

NUTRITIONAL INFORMATION

Energy	Fat	Carbohydrates	Protein	Sodium
178 calories	13.5 g	6.3 g	9.3 g	241 mg

SCRAMBLED EGGS WITH COTTAGE CHEESE AND CORIANDER

Preparation Time	Total Time	Yield
5 minutes	15 minutes	4 servings

INGREDIENTS

- 4 whole eggs (about 60 g each)
- 4 egg whites (about 40 g each)
- 2 tablespoons (30 ml) milk
- 2 tablespoons (30 g) mayonnaise
- 2 tablespoons (30 ml) olive oil
- 1 teaspoon (3 g) garlic, minced
- 1/2 cup (110 g) cottage cheese
- 2 tablespoons (7 g) fresh coriander leaves or cilantro, chopped
- 1/4 teaspoon (1.5 g) kosher salt
- 1/4 teaspoon (0.5 g) ground coriander seeds
- 1/4 teaspoon (0.5 g) lemon pepper

METHOD

- Whisk the eggs in a bowl, then stir in milk and mayonnaise. Mix until well-blended.
- Heat oil in a large non-stick pan or skillet over medium flame. Stir-fry garlic for 2-3 minutes or until aromatic.
- Add in egg mixture, cottage cheese, and coriander leaves; cook for 2-3 minutes, stirring often. Season with salt, ground coriander, and lemon pepper. Remove from heat.

- Transfer to a serving dish.
- Serve and enjoy.

NUTRITIONAL INFORMATION

Energy	Fat	Carbohydrates	Protein	Sodium
177 calories	11.5 g	3.9 g	14.1 g	254 mg

SCRAMBLED EGGS WITH SUN-DRIED TOMATOES ON TOAST

Preparation Time	Total Time	Yield
5 minutes	15 minutes	4 servings

INGREDIENTS

- 3 whole eggs (about 60 g each)
- 3 egg whites (about 40 g each)
- 1/4 cup (60 ml) milk
- 2 tablespoons (30 ml) olive oil
- 1 medium (110 g) white onion, chopped
- 2 tablespoons (15 g) sun dried tomatoes in oil, drained and chopped
- 2 tablespoons (15 g) parmesan cheese, grated
- 2 tablespoons (7 f) fresh basil, chopped
- 4 wholegrain or multigrain bread slices (about 30 g each), toasted
- Salt and freshly ground black pepper
- Fresh basil, for garnish

METHOD

- Whisk the eggs and stir in milk in a medium bowl.
- Heat oil in a large non-stick pan or skillet over medium flame. Stir-fry onion and sun-dried tomatoes for 2-3 minutes.
- Pour the egg mixture, basil, and parmesan; cook, stirring for 2-3 minutes.
- Spoon about 3 tablespoons of egg mixture on top of

each toast and garnish with fresh basil.

- Serve and enjoy!

NUTRITIONAL INFORMATION

Energy	Fat	Carbohydrates	Protein	Sodium
218 calories	10.8 g	16.4 g	14.4 g	268 mg

SCRAMBLED EGGS WITH CHERRY TOMATOES AND CHIVES

Preparation Time	Total Time	Yield
5 minutes	15 minutes	4 servings

INGREDIENTS

- 4 whole eggs (about 60 g each)
- 2 egg whites (about 40 g each)
- 1/4 cup (60 ml) milk
- 1 teaspoon (2 g) paprika
- 1/2 teaspoon (1 g) garlic powder
- 2 tablespoons (30 ml) olive oil
- 1 medium (110 g) white onion, chopped
- 1 cup (150 g) cherry tomatoes, halved
- 4 tablespoons (7 g) chopped fresh chives, divided
- Salt and freshly ground black pepper

METHOD

- Whisk together the eggs, milk, paprika, and garlic powder in a medium bowl.
- Heat oil in a large non-stick pan or skillet over medium heat. Stir-fry onion and cherry tomatoes until aromatic, about 2-3 minutes.
- Add the beaten egg mixture and 2 tablespoons of chives; cook, stirring for 3-4 minutes.
- Transfer to a serving plate and sprinkle with remaining chives.
- Serve and enjoy.

NUTRITIONAL INFORMATION

Energy	Fat	Carbohydrates	Protein	Sodium
165 calories	11.8 g	6.1 g	9.6 g	245 mg

CHEESY BROCCOLI AND ONION QUICHE

Preparation Time	Total Time	Yield
10 minutes	60 minutes	8 servings

INGREDIENTS

- 2 tablespoons (30 ml) olive oil
- 1/3 cup (55 g) shallots, chopped
- 1 tablespoon (9 g) garlic, minced
- 2 cups (260 g) fresh broccoli, chopped
- 1 (9-inch) pie crust, unbaked
- 1/4 cup (30 g) mozzarella cheese, shredded
- 1/4 cup (30 g) cheddar cheese, grated
- 6 whole eggs (about 60 g each)
- 4 egg whites (about 40 g)
- 2/3 cup (170 ml) milk
- 1 tablespoon (15 g) butter, melted
- Salt and freshly ground black pepper

METHOD

- Preheat and set your oven to 350 F (175 C).
- Heat oil in a large non-stick pan or skillet over medium flame. Stir-fry the shallots and garlic for 2-3 minutes or until aromatic.
- Add the broccoli; cook, stirring occasionally until soft.
- Transfer the cooked vegetables into the pie crust. Sprinkle with cheddar and mozzarella.
- Whisk the eggs, and then stir in milk and melted butter in a medium bowl. Season to taste.
- Pour the egg mixture over broccoli and cheese. Bake

in the oven for 30 to 40 minutes, or until center has set fully.
- Cool the quiche slightly before serving.
- Enjoy.

NUTRITIONAL INFORMATION

Energy	Fat	Carbohydrates	Protein	Sodium
247 calories	16.6 g	14.7 g	10.5 g	244 mg

LEFTOVER SALMON AND CHERRY TOMATO QUICHE

Preparation Time	Total Time	Yield
10 minutes	60 minutes	8 servings

INGREDIENTS

- 2 tablespoons (30 ml) olive oil
- 1 medium (110 g) red onion, chopped
- 1 teaspoon (3 g) garlic, minced
- 1 cup (150 g) cherry tomatoes, halved
- 10 oz. (300 g) leftover baked salmon, cut into thin strips
- 1 teaspoon (5 g) dill weed, chopped
- 1 (9-inch) pie crust, unbaked
- 1/3 cup (40 g) cheddar cheese, grated
- 2 tablespoons (15 g) parmesan, grated
- 6 whole eggs (about 60 g each)
- 4 egg whites (about 40 g each)
- 2/3 cup (165 ml) milk
- 1/2 teaspoon (2.5 g) kosher salt
- 1/2 teaspoon (1 g) lemon pepper

METHOD

- Preheat and set your oven to 350 F (175 C).
- Heat oil in a large non-stick pan or skillet over medium flame. Add the onion and garlic, stir-fry for about 2-3 minutes.
- Add the cherry tomatoes; cook, stirring occasionally until soft.

- Add the salmon and dill; mix well. Remove from heat.
- Transfer the vegetable-salmon mixture onto the pie crust. Sprinkle with cheddar and parmesan.
- Whisk the eggs in a medium bowl, and then stir in milk. Season with salt and lemon pepper.
- Pour the egg mixture into the pie crust. Bake in the preheated oven for about 30 to 40 minutes or until center has set fully.
- Cool the quiche slightly before serving.
- Enjoy.

NUTRITIONAL INFORMATION

Energy	Fat	Carbohydrates	Protein	Sodium
260 calories	16.6 g	11.8 g	16.5 g	232 mg

CHICKEN AND VEGETABLE QUICHE WITH MOZZARELLA

Preparation Time	Total Time	Yield
10 minutes	60 minutes	8 servings

INGREDIENTS

- 2 tablespoons (30 ml) olive oil
- 1 medium (110 g) red onion, chopped
- 1 teaspoon (3 g) garlic, minced
- 8 oz. (250 g) leftover roasted chicken, shredded
- 1 cup (150 g) frozen mixed vegetables, thawed
- 1 tablespoon (3.5 g) fresh rosemary, chopped
- 1 tablespoon (3.5 g) fresh parsley, chopped
- 1 (10-inch) pie crust, unbaked
- 6 whole eggs (about 60 g each)
- 4 egg whites (about 40 g each)
- 3/4 cup (185 ml) milk
- 1/2 cup (60 g) mozzarella cheese, grated
- 1/2 teaspoon (2.5 g) kosher salt
- 1/2 teaspoon (1 g) lemon pepper

METHOD

- Preheat and set your oven to 350 F (175 C).
- Heat oil in a large non-stick pan or skillet over medium flame. Add the onion and garlic, stir-fry for about 2-3 minutes.
- Add the chicken, mixed vegetables, rosemary, and parsley; cook for about 3 minutes, stirring

occasionally. Remove from the heat and spoon mixture over the pie crust. Set aside.
- Whisk together the eggs and milk in a medium bowl. Season with salt and lemon pepper.
- Pour the egg mixture over the chicken and mixed vegetables. Bake in the oven for 20-25 minutes.
- Sprinkle with mozzarella and cook for another 15-20 minutes.
- Cool the quiche slightly before serving.
- Enjoy.

NUTRITIONAL INFORMATION

Energy	Fat	Carbohydrates	Protein	Sodium
255 calories	14.1 g	14.1 g	17.6 g	219 mg

HERBED MUSHROOM AND CHEESE QUICHE

Preparation Time	Total Time	Yield
10 minutes	60 minutes	8 servings

INGREDIENTS

- 2 tablespoons (30 ml) olive oil
- 1 medium (110 g) white onion, chopped
- 1 teaspoon (3 g) garlic, minced
- 1 cup (150 g) button mushrooms, chopped
- 1/2 teaspoon (1 g) Italian seasoning
- 1 (9-inch) pie crust, unbaked
- 4 whole eggs (about 60 g each)
- 4 egg whites (about 40 g each)
- 1/2 cup (125 ml) milk
- 1/4 cup (30 g) mozzarella cheese, grated
- 1/4 cup (30 g) cheddar cheese, grated
- Salt and freshly ground black pepper

METHOD

- Preheat and set your oven to 350 F (175 C).
- Heat oil in a large non-stick pan or skillet over medium flame. Add the onion and garlic, stir-fry for about 2-3 minutes.
- Add the mushrooms and Italian seasoning; cook for about 2-3 minutes, stirring occasionally. Remove from heat and spoon mixture onto the pie crust.
- Whisk together the eggs and milk in a medium bowl. Season to taste.
- Pour the egg mixture over mushrooms. Bake in the

oven for 20-25 minutes. Sprinkle with cheddar and mozzarella and cook for another 15-20 minutes.

- Cool the quiche slightly before serving.
- Enjoy.

NUTRITIONAL INFORMATION

Energy	Fat	Carbohydrates	Protein	Sodium
256 calories	15.2 g	22.5 g	8.3 g	258 mg

SPINACH RICOTTA AND HERB QUICHE

Preparation Time	Total Time	Yield
10 minutes	60 minutes	8 servings

INGREDIENTS

- 2 tablespoons (30 g) butter
- 1/3 cup (55 g) shallots, chopped
- 1 teaspoon (3 g) garlic, minced
- 3 cups (90 g) baby spinach
- 1/4 teaspoon (0.5 g) dried basil
- 1/4 teaspoon (0.5 g) dried oregano
- 1 (9x9-inch) pie crust, unbaked
- 5 whole eggs (about 60 g each)
- 4 egg whites (about 40 g each)
- 1 cup (220 g) ricotta cheese
- 1/4 cup (60 ml) milk
- Freshly ground black pepper

METHOD

- Preheat and set your oven to 350 F (175 C). Put the crust in a baking dish.
- Heat oil in a large non-stick pan or skillet over medium flame. Add the shallots and garlic, stir-fry for 2-3 minutes.
- Add the spinach, basil, and oregano. Cook for about 2-3 minutes, stirring occasionally. Remove from heat. Spoon vegetables onto the pie crust.
- Whisk together the eggs, ricotta, and milk in a medium bowl. Season with pepper to taste.

- Pour the egg mixture over vegetables, spreading evenly. Bake in the preheated oven for about 35–40 minutes or until the center is set fully.
- Cool the quiche slightly before cutting into portions.
- Serve and enjoy.

NUTRITIONAL INFORMATION

Energy	Fat	Carbohydrates	Protein	Sodium
276 calories	15.7 g	24.0 g	10.7 g	295 mg

ZUCCHINI TOMATO AND OLIVE QUICHE

Preparation Time	Total Time	Yield
10 minutes	60 minutes	8 servings

INGREDIENTS

- 1 medium (110 g) red onion, thinly sliced into rounds
- 1 medium (200 g) zucchini, thinly sliced into rounds
- 1 (150 g) tomato, thinly sliced into rounds
- 8 (10 g) black olives, sliced
- 1/2 teaspoon (1 g) Italian seasoning
- 1/4 cup (30 g) parmesan cheese
- 1 (9-inch) pie crust, unbaked
- 4 whole eggs (about 60 g each)
- 4 egg whites (about 40 g each)
- 1/2 cup (125 ml) milk
- Salt and freshly ground black pepper

METHOD

- Preheat and set your oven to 350 F (175 C).
- Arrange the sliced onion, zucchini, tomato, and olives onto the pie crust. Then sprinkle with Italian seasoning and ¼ cup parmesan cheese.
- Whisk together the eggs and milk in a mixing bowl. Season to taste.
- Pour the egg mixture over vegetables. Bake in the preheated oven for about 35-40 minutes or until the center is set.
- Cool the quiche slightly before serving.
- Serve and enjoy.

NUTRITIONAL INFORMATION

Energy	Fat	Carbohydrates	Protein	Sodium
230 calories	11.8 g	24.2 g	8.0 g	324 mg

PEPPER ONION AND CHEESE OMELETTE

Preparation Time	Total Time	Yield
5 minutes	15 minutes	5 servings

INGREDIENTS

- 4 whole eggs (about 60 g each)
- 3 egg whites (about 40 g each)
- 2 tablespoons (30 ml) olive oil, divided
- 1 medium (110 g) red onion, julienned
- 1/2 medium (60 g) green bell pepper, julienned
- 1/2 medium (60 g) red bell pepper, julienned
- 1/2 medium (60 g) yellow bell pepper, julienned
- 1/4 cup (30 g) cheddar cheese, grated
- 2 tablespoons (7 g) fresh parsley, chopped
- Salt and freshly ground black pepper
- Fresh parsley, for garnish

METHOD

- Whisk the eggs together in a mixing bowl and season to taste. Set aside.
- Stir-fry onion and bell peppers with 1 tablespoon oil in a non-stick pan over medium flame for about 2-3 minutes. Transfer vegetables mixture to a clean plate and set aside.
- Add the remaining 1 tablespoon oil in the same pan. Then pour in the beaten egg and cook for about 2-3 minutes. When the egg mixture starts to set at the bottom of the pan, lightly lift the cooked edge of the egg using a spatula, letting the uncooked egg mixture flow to the edge. Cook for another 1-2 minutes.

- Top half part of the egg with sautéed vegetables. Sprinkle with cheddar cheese and parsley. Gently lift the other half of egg over the cooked vegetables. Cook over low flame for 2-3 minutes more.
- Slide the vegetable omelette into a serving plate. Garnish with fresh parsley.
- Serve and enjoy!

NUTRITIONAL INFORMATION

Energy	Fat	Carbohydrates	Protein	Sodium
176 calories	12.1 g	8.1 g	10.1 g	236 mg

CHICKEN HAM PEPPER AND CHEESE OMELETTE

Preparation Time	Total Time	Yield
5 minutes	15 minutes	4 servings

INGREDIENTS

- 3 whole eggs (about 60 g each)
- 3 egg whites (about 40 g each)
- 2 tablespoons (30 ml) olive oil, divided
- 1/2 medium (60 g) red bell pepper, diced
- 1/2 medium (60 g) green bell pepper, diced
- 4 oz. (125 g) chicken ham, diced
- 2 tablespoons (7 g) green onion, chopped
- 2 tablespoons (15 g) cheddar cheese, grated
- Freshly ground black pepper, to taste

METHOD

- In a medium bowl, beat the eggs together and season to taste.
- Heat 1 tablespoon of oil in a skillet or non-stick pan over medium flame. Stir-fry the red and green bell pepper until soft.
- Add the chicken ham and cook for another 2 minutes. Transfer mixture to a clean plate. Set aside.
- In the same pan, add the remaining 1 tablespoon oil. Then pour the beaten egg and cook for about 2 minutes. Gently lift the edge of the egg mixture with a spatula, let the uncooked egg mixture flow to the edges of the pan. Cook for about 2 minutes.
- Top half of the egg with chicken ham and vegetable mixture. Sprinkle with green onion. Slowly lift the other

side over the ham and vegetable mixture. Sprinkle with cheese and cook further 1–2 minutes.
- Transfer to a serving dish.
- Serve and enjoy.

NUTRITIONAL INFORMATION

Energy	Fat	Carbohydrates	Protein	Sodium
188 calories	13.6g	5.9 g	11.8 g	269 mg

MUSHROOM OMELETTE WITH BASIL

Preparation Time	Total Time	Yield
5minutes	15 minutes	4 servings

INGREDIENTS

- 4 whole eggs (about 60 g each)
- 2 egg whites (about 40 g each)
- 1 tablespoon (15 g) mayonnaise
- 2 tablespoons (30 ml) olive oil
- 1 medium (110 g) onion, thinly sliced
- 1 teaspoon (3 g) garlic, crushed
- 1 cup (150 g) button mushroom, sliced
- 1/4 cup (15 g) fresh basil, chopped
- Salt and freshly ground black pepper
- Tomato slices, to serve
- Chopped fresh basil, for garnish

METHOD

- Whisk together the eggs and mayonnaise in a medium mixing bowl. Season with salt and pepper.
- Heat the oil in a non-stick pan, stir-fry onion and garlic for about 2-3 minutes.
- Add the mushrooms and basil; cook, stirring for 2 minutes.
- Pour in the beaten eggs and cook for 4-5 minutes, turning once to cook the other side.
- Transfer to a serving dish. Sprinkle with chopped basil, if desired.
- Serve with tomato slices on side.

- Enjoy.

NUTRITIONAL INFORMATION

Energy	Fat	Carbohydrates	Protein	Sodium
162 calories	12.7 g	4.8 g	8.3 g	254 mg

ASPARAGUS AND PARMESAN OMELETTE

Preparation Time	Total Time	Yield
15 minutes	15 minutes	4 servings

INGREDIENTS

- 4 whole eggs (about 60 g each)
- 4 egg whites (about 40 g each)
- 2 tablespoons (30 ml) olive oil
- 1 medium (110 g) onion, thinly sliced
- 1 teaspoon (3 g) garlic, crushed
- 1 cup (130 g) asparagus tips, trimmed
- 2 tablespoons (15 g) capers, rinsed and drained
- 1/4 teaspoon (0.5 g) dried rosemary
- 2 tablespoons (15 g) parmesan cheese
- Salt and freshly ground black pepper
- Fresh parsley, for garnish

METHOD

- Beat the eggs in a medium mixing bowl and season with pepper.
- Heat oil in a non-stick pan or skillet over medium flame. Stir-fry onion and garlic for about 2-3 minutes.
- Add the asparagus, capers, and rosemary; cook, stirring for 5 minutes or until asparagus are tender. Transfer vegetable mixture to a clean plate and set aside.
- Using the same pan, heat the remaining 1 tablespoon oil. Pour the beaten eggs and cook for about 2 minutes. Gently lift the edge of the egg mixture with

a spatula, let the uncooked egg mixture flow to the edges of the pan; cook for about 2 minutes.

- Top half of the egg with sautéed asparagus mixture. Slowly lift the other side to cover the filling; cook for 2 minutes more.
- Slide the omelette into a serving plate. Sprinkle with grated parmesan cheese and garnish with fresh parsley.
- Serve and enjoy.

NUTRITIONAL INFORMATION

Energy	Fat	Carbohydrates	Protein	Sodium
170 calories	12.6 g	4.8 g	10.9 g	262 mg

BREAKFAST OMELETTE WITH MUSHROOM AND TOMATO

Preparation Time	Total Time	Yield
5 minutes	15 minutes	3 servings

INGREDIENTS

- 3 whole eggs (about 60 g each)
- 3 egg whites (about 40 g each)
- 2 tablespoons (30 ml) milk
- 1/2 teaspoon (1 g) garlic powder
- 1 tablespoon (15 g) butter
- 1 cup (150 g) button mushrooms, sliced
- 1 medium (125 g) tomato, sliced
- Salt and freshly ground black pepper

METHOD

- Whisk the eggs and milk together in a mixing bowl. Season to taste.
- Heat butter in a non-stick pan over medium flame. Stir-fry the mushrooms and tomato until soft. Transfer vegetable mixture to a clean plate and set aside.
- In the same pan, cook the beaten eggs for about 2 minutes. Gently lift the edge of the egg mixture with a spatula, let the uncooked egg mixture flow to the edges of the pan; cook for about 3-4 minutes.
- Top half of the egg with mushroom-tomato mixture. Slowly lift the other side to cover the filling; cook for 2-3 minutes more.
- Slide the omelette into a serving dish.

- Serve and enjoy.

NUTRITIONAL INFORMATION

Energy	Fat	Carbohydrates	Protein	Sodium
124 calories	8.4g	2.4 g	10.1 g	175 mg

BEAN AND CORIANDER OMELETTE

Preparation Time	Total Time	Yield
5 minutes	15 minutes	3 servings

INGREDIENTS

- 3 whole eggs (about 60 g each)
- 3 egg whites (about 40 g each)
- 1 Tbsp. (15 g) butter
- 2/3 cup (165 g) baked chili beans
- 1 tablespoon (3.5 g) fresh coriander, chopped
- Salt and freshly ground black pepper

METHOD

- Whisk together the eggs in a mixing bowl and season to taste.
- Heat the butter in a non-stick pan over medium flame.
- Pour the egg and cook for about 2 minutes. Gently lift the edge of the egg mixture with a spatula, let the uncooked egg mixture flow to the edges of the pan; cook for about 2 minutes.
- Top half of the egg with baked chili beans. Sprinkle with chopped coriander. Slowly lift the egg to cover the bean filling and cook for another 2 minutes.
- Transfer to a serving dish.
- Serve and enjoy.

NUTRITIONAL INFORMATION

Energy	Fat	Carbohydrates	Protein	Sodium
199 calories	11.2 g	12.6 g	12.3 g	175 mg

HERBED SALMON AND TOMATO OMELETTE

Preparation Time	Total Time	Yield
5 minutes	15 minutes	4 servings

INGREDIENTS

- 4 whole eggs (about 60 g each)
- 3 egg whites (about 40 g each)
- 2 tablespoons (30 ml) olive oil, divided
- 1/3 cup shallots, chopped
- 1 teaspoon (3 g) garlic, minced
- 1 cup (150 g) cherry tomatoes, quartered
- 2 oz. (60 g) smoked salmon, chopped
- 2 tablespoons (7 g) fresh parsley, chopped
- Salt and freshly ground black pepper

METHOD

- In a medium bowl, beat the eggs together and season to taste.
- Heat 1 tablespoon oil in a skillet or non-stick pan over medium flame. Add the shallots and garlic, stir-fry for 2-3 minutes.
- Add the cherry tomatoes and salmon; cook, stirring for 2-3 minutes. Transfer mixture to a clean plate and then set aside.
- In the same pan, add the remaining 1 tablespoon oil. Then pour the beaten egg and cook for about 2 minutes. Gently lift the edge of the egg mixture with a spatula, let the uncooked egg mixture flow to the edges of the pan. Cook for about 1-2 minutes.
- Top half of the egg with tomato-salmon mixture and

then sprinkle with parsley. Gently lift the other side to cover the filling; cook for 2 minutes more.
- Transfer to a serving dish.
- Serve and enjoy.

NUTRITIONAL INFORMATION

Energy	Fat	Carbohydrates	Protein	Sodium
173 calories	12.2 g	5.2 g	11.6 g	305 mg

MEDITERRANEAN-STYLE OMELETTE

Preparation Time	Total Time	Yield
5 minutes	15 minutes	4 servings

INGREDIENTS

- 3 whole eggs (about 60 g each)
- 3 egg whites (about 40 g each)
- 2 tablespoons (30 ml) olive oil, divided
- 1 medium (110 g) onion, chopped
- 1 teaspoon (3 g) garlic, crushed
- 1 medium (125 g) tomato, diced
- 1 medium (120 g) green bell pepper, chopped
- 1/2 cup (110 g) feta cheese, diced
- 2 tablespoons (7 g) fresh basil, chopped
- Salt and freshly ground black pepper

METHOD

- In a medium bowl, beat the eggs and season to taste.
- Heat 1 tablespoon oil in a skillet or non-stick pan over medium flame; stir-fry onion and garlic for 2-3 minutes.
- Add the tomato and green bell pepper; cook until soft, stirring frequently. Transfer mixture into a clean plate and set aside.
- Using the same pan, heat the remaining 1 tablespoon oil. Then pour the beaten egg and cook for about 2 minutes. Gently lift the edge of the egg mixture with a spatula, let the uncooked egg mixture flow to the edges of the pan; cook for about 2 minutes.
- Top half of the egg with tomato mixture, feta cheese,

and basil. Gently lift the other side over the vegetable and feta filling; cook for 2 minutes more.
- Slide the omelette into a serving dish.
- Serve and enjoy.

NUTRITIONAL INFORMATION

Energy	Fat	Carbohydrates	Protein	Sodium
197 calories	14.5 g	7.5 g	10.5 g	284 mg

PEPPER BROCCOLI AND CHEESE OMELETTE

Preparation Time	Total Time	Yield
5 minutes	15 minutes	4 servings

INGREDIENTS

- 4 whole eggs (about 60 g each)
- 4 egg whites (about 40 g each)
- 2 tablespoons (30 ml) olive oil, divided
- 1 medium (110 g) onion, chopped
- 1 medium (120 g) red bell pepper
- 1 cup (130 g) broccoli, coarsely chopped
- 1/4 cup (30 g) mozzarella cheese, diced
- 2 tablespoons (15 g) cheddar cheese
- Salt and freshly ground black pepper
- Fresh parsley, to serve

METHOD

- In a medium bowl, beat the eggs together and season to taste.
- Heat 1 tablespoon oil in a skillet or non-stick pan over medium flame, stir-fry onion for 2-3 minutes.
- Add the bell pepper and broccoli; cook until tender, stirring frequently. Transfer vegetables into a clean plate and set aside.
- Using the same pan, heat the remaining 1 tablespoon oil. Then pour the beaten egg and cook for about 2 minutes. Gently lift the edge of the egg mixture with a spatula, let the uncooked egg mixture flow to the edges of the pan; cook for about 1-2 minutes.
- Top half of the egg with vegetable mixture, mozzarella,

and cheddar. Gently lift the other side to cover the vegetable and cheese filling; cook for 2-3 minutes more.
- Slide the omelette into a serving dish and garnish with fresh parsley.
- Serve and enjoy.

NUTRITIONAL INFORMATION

Energy	Fat	Carbohydrates	Protein	Sodium
183 calories	13.1 g	7.0 g	10.9 g	228 mg

SHRIMP AND CHEDDAR OMELETTE WITH CHIVES

Preparation Time	Total Time	Yield
5 minutes	15 minutes	4 servings

INGREDIENTS

- 4 whole eggs (about 60 g each)
- 4 egg whites (about 40 g each)
- 2 tablespoons (30 ml) olive oil, divided
- 1 medium (110 g) onion, chopped
- 1 medium (125 g) tomato, sliced
- 1 (3 g) clove garlic, crushed
- 4 oz. (125 g) small shrimps
- 1/4 cup (30 g) cheddar cheese, grated
- 1/4 cup (15 g) chives, chopped
- Salt and freshly ground black pepper

METHOD

- In a medium bowl, beat the eggs together and season to taste.
- Heat 1 tablespoon oil in a skillet or non-stick pan over medium flame. Stir-fry onion, tomato, and garlic for 3 minutes.
- Add the shrimps; cook for 2-3 minutes, stirring constantly until it turned pink. Transfer mixture into a clean plate and then set aside.
- Using the same pan, heat the remaining 1 tablespoon oil. Then pour the egg and cook for about 2 minutes. Gently lift the edge of the egg mixture with a spatula, let the uncooked egg mixture flow to the edges of the pan; cook for about 2 minutes.
- Top half of the egg with shrimps and sprinkle with

cheddar and chives. Gently lift the other side to cover the shrimp filling; cook for another 2-3 minutes.
- Slide the omelette into a serving dish.
- Serve and enjoy.

NUTRITIONAL INFORMATION

Energy	Fat	Carbohydrates	Protein	Sodium
171 calories	11.7 g	4.0 g	13.7 g	334 mg

PEPPER AND MUSHROOM OMELETTE WITH HERBS

Preparation Time	Total Time	Yield
5 minutes	15 minutes	3 servings

INGREDIENTS

- 3 whole eggs (about 60 g each)
- 3 egg whites (about 40 g each)
- 2 tablespoons (30 ml) olive oil, divided
- 1 medium (110 g) onion, chopped
- 1 teaspoon (3 g) garlic, minced
- 1/2 medium (60 g) yellow bell pepper, thinly sliced
- 1/2 cup (75 g) button mushrooms, thinly sliced
- 2 tablespoons (7 g) dill weed, chopped
- Salt and freshly ground black pepper
- Chopped fresh dill weed, for garnish

METHOD

- Beat the eggs together in a medium bowl and season to taste.
- Heat 1 tablespoon oil in a skillet or non-stick pan over medium flame. Add the onion and garlic, stir-fry for about 2-3 minutes.
- Add the bell pepper, mushrooms, and dill. Cook for 2-3 minutes, stirring frequently. Transfer mixture into a clean plate and set aside.
- Using the same pan, heat the remaining 1 tablespoon oil. Then pour the beaten egg and cook for about 2

minutes. Gently lift the edge of the egg mixture with a spatula, let the uncooked egg mixture flow to the edges of the pan; cook for about 1-2 minutes.

- Top half of the egg with pepper-mushroom mixture. Gently lift the other side over the vegetable filling; cook for 2 minutes more.
- Slide the omelette into a serving dish and garnish with chopped dill.
- Serve and enjoy.

NUTRITIONAL INFORMATION

Energy	Fat	Carbohydrates	Protein	Sodium
188 calories	13.9 g	6.8 g	10.4 g	294 mg

SMOKED SALMON AND DILL OMELETTE

Preparation Time	Total Time	Yield
5 minutes	15 minutes	3 servings

INGREDIENTS

- 4 whole eggs (about 60 g each)
- 3 egg whites (about 40 g each)
- 2 tablespoons (45 g) sour cream
- 2 tablespoons (30 ml) olive oil, divided
- 1 medium (110 g) onion, chopped
- 1 teaspoon (3 g) garlic, minced
- 2 oz. (60 g) smoked salmon, thinly sliced
- 1 tablespoon (7 g) fresh dill, chopped
- Salt and freshly ground black pepper

METHOD

- In a medium bowl, whisk together the eggs and sour cream. Season to taste and set aside.
- Heat 1 tablespoon oil in a skillet or non-stick pan over medium flame. Add the onion and garlic, stir-fry for about 2-3 minutes.
- Add the smoked salmon; cook, stirring for 2 minutes. Transfer mixture into a plate and set aside.
- Using the same pan, heat the remaining 1 tablespoon oil. Then pour the beaten egg and cook for about 2 minutes. Gently lift the edge of the egg mixture with a spatula, let the uncooked egg mixture flow to the edges of the pan. Cook for about 1-2 minutes.
- Top half of the egg with smoked salmon and dill. Gently lift the other side over the salmon filling; cook

for 2 minutes more.
- Slide the omelette into a serving dish.
- Serve and enjoy.

NUTRITIONAL INFORMATION

Energy	Fat	Carbohydrates	Protein	Sodium
186 calories	14.0 g	4.2 g	11.6 g	370 mg

EGG SANDWICH WITH AVOCADO AND TOMATO

Preparation Time	Total Time	Yield
10 minutes	20 minutes	4 servings

INGREDIENTS

- 4 poached eggs (about 60 g each)
- 1/2 medium (100 g) avocado
- 1 large (150 g) tomato
- 1 teaspoon (2 g) sweet paprika
- 4 (30 g) wholegrain bread slices, toasted
- Salt and freshly ground black pepper

METHOD

- Cut tomato into thin slices then set aside.
- Mash the avocado in a small bowl and season to taste.
- Top each bread toast with mashed avocado, sliced tomatoes, and 1 poached egg. Sprinkle eggs with paprika and season to taste.
- Place the toasts into a serving dish.
- Serve and enjoy.

NUTRITIONAL INFORMATION

Energy	Fat	Carbohydrates	Protein	Sodium
192 calories	10.3 g	15.9 g	10.1 g	195 mg

BONUS EGG
DESSERT AND
SNACK RECIPES

ASIAN-STYLE EGG TARTS

Preparation Time	Total Time	Yield
15 minutes	55 minutes	24 servings

INGREDIENTS

- 1 ¼ cup (315 ml) water
- 3/4 cup (100 g) granulated sugar
- 8 whole eggs (about 60 g each)
- 1 cup (250 ml) evaporated milk
- 1 teaspoon (5 ml) vanilla extract
- 16 ounces (450 g) pastry dough, unbaked

METHOD

- Preheat and set your oven to 400 F (200 C).
- In a small pot or saucepan, combine the water and sugar. Bring to a boil over medium-high flame; cook until sugar is dissolved. Turn off the heat. Set aside and let it cool.
- Whisk the eggs in a mixing bowl, and then stir in evaporated milk and cooled syrup; mix until blended well.
- Form the pastry dough into 1 1/2 inch balls, and press them onto muffin molds so that it covers the bottom, and goes up to the sides. Use a fork or your 2 fingers to form the edge. Strain the egg mixture through a fine sieve and fill the tart shells, about 3/4 full.
- Bake in the preheated oven until golden and the filling has puffed a little, about 25-30 minutes. Cool the egg tarts on a wire rack.
- Serve and enjoy.

NUTRITIONAL INFORMATION

Energy	Fat	Carbohydrates	Protein	Sodium
259 calories	13.6 g	30.1 g	4.5 g	253 mg

CARAMEL CUSTARD PUDDING

Preparation Time	Total Time	Yield
15 minutes	5 hours 15 minutes	6 servings

INGREDIENTS

For the Caramel Sauce:
- 1/4 cup (60 ml) water
- 1 cup (220 g) light brown sugar

For the Custard:
- 8 egg yolks (about 20 g each)
- 4 whole eggs (about 60 g each)
- 1 (14.5 fl. oz. or 406 ml) can evaporated milk
- 1 (15 fl. oz. or 420 ml) can condensed milk
- 1 teaspoon (5 ml) vanilla extract

You will need:
- 6 (4-ounce) ramekins or flan molds
- Steamer
- Water for the steamer

METHOD

- Prepare the caramel by combining the water and sugar in a small saucepan. Bring to a boil over medium-high flame. Lower the heat to medium-low; cook until the sugar caramelizes and becomes golden brown in color. Do not to overcook or else your caramel will taste bitter. Pour the caramel to the ramekins and spread evenly. Set aside.
- Fill your steamer with just enough amount of water and bring to a boil over medium flame.
- Meanwhile, whisk together the eggs, sweetened condensed milk, evaporated milk, and vanilla extract in a large bowl. Stir gently until blended well. Strain the

mixture into the prepared ramekins. Cover with foil and then put in the steamer.

- Reduce heat to low and steam, covered until the custard is firm, about 45 minutes to 1 hour. Set aside to cool at room temperature then refrigerate for 4 hours or until ready to serve.
- *To serve:* Run a knife along the sides of each custard to loosen them up. Invert into serving plates.
- Serve and enjoy.

NUTRITIONAL INFORMATION

Energy	Fat	Carbohydrates	Protein	Sodium
280 calories	0.0 g	37.2 g	9.3 g	114 mg

BAKED CUSTARD PUDDING WITH RASPBERRIES

Preparation Time	Total Time	Yield
15 minutes	5 hours 15 minutes	8 servings

INGREDIENTS

For the Caramel Sauce:

- 1/4 cup (60 ml) water
- 3/4 cup (165 g) white sugar
- 1/4 cup (60 g) maple syrup

For the Custard:

- 4 whole eggs (about 60 g each)
- 8 egg yolks (about 20 g each)
- 1 1/2 cups (375 ml) whole milk

- 1 can (15 fl. oz. or 420 ml) sweetened condensed milk
- 1 tsp. (5 ml) vanilla extract

To Serve:

- 1 cup (125 g) fresh raspberries

You will need:

- 8 (3-ounce) ramekins or flan molds
- Hot water

METHOD

- Preheat and set your oven to 350 F (175 C).
- Combine the water, sugar, and 1/4 cup maple syrup in a saucepan. Bring to a boil over medium-high flame. Lower heat to medium-low; cook until the sugar caramelizes and becomes golden brown in color. Pour into eight ramekins and spread evenly. Set aside.
- Whisk together the eggs in a bowl until lightly beaten. Stir in whole milk, sweetened condensed milk, and vanilla extract until incorporated well. Pour the custard

mixture over caramel in ramekins.

- Place ramekins in a baking dish. Pour just enough hot water into the baking dish to cover halfway up the sides of ramekins.
- Bake in the oven for 45 minutes or until a skewer inserted in the center of the custard comes out clean. Remove from heat. Take out the ramekins from baking dish and cool them at room temperature. Chill for 4 hours before serving.
- *To serve:* Invert each ramekin into individual plates and top with fresh raspberries.
- Enjoy.

NUTRITIONAL INFORMATION

Energy	Fat	Carbohydrates	Protein	Sodium
297 calories	9.8 g	44.1 g	9.1 g	113 mg

CARAMELIZED ORANGE CREAM CUSTARD

Preparation Time	Total Time	Yield
15 minutes	5 hours 15 minutes	10 servings

INGREDIENTS

For the Caramel:

- 3 Tbsp. (45 ml) water
- 1 cup (220 g) white sugar
- 1 Tbsp. (15 g) orange zest, finely grated

For the Custard:

- 8 egg yolks (about 20 g each)
- 4 whole eggs (about 60 g each)
- 1 (15 fl. oz. or 420 ml) can sweetened condensed milk
- 1 (14.5 fl. oz. or 406 ml) can evaporated milk
- 1 tsp. (5 ml) orange extract

You will need:

- Custard molds or ramekins
- Water, for the steamer

METHOD

- Prepare the caramel by combining water and sugar in a saucepan; bring to a boil. Reduce the heat to low then add the orange zest; cook until the sugar caramelizes and turns golden brown in color. Make sure not to overcook or else your caramel will give you a bitter taste. Pour the caramel into the custard molds or ramekins and spread the caramel evenly. Set aside.
- Fill the bottom part of your steamer with just enough water. Cover with lid and bring to a simmer over medium flame.
- Combine the eggs, condensed milk, evaporated milk, and orange extract in a large bowl. Strain the mixture into the prepared custard molds. Cover with foil and

put them in the steamer.

- Check if the water is simmering before you put them in. Cover with lid. Reduce heat to low and steam until the custard is firm, about 45 minutes to 1 hour. Let them cool at room temperature, and then chill for at least 4 hours.
- *To serve:* Loosen them up by running a knife at the sides then invert into serving plates.
- Serve and enjoy.

NUTRITIONAL INFORMATION

Energy	Fat	Carbohydrates	Protein	Sodium
259 calories	10.8 g	32.1 g	9.3 g	112 mg

CREAMY VANILLA CUSTARD WITH CHERRY COMPOTE

Preparation Time	Total Time	Yield
15 minutes	5 hours 15 minutes	10 servings

INGREDIENTS

For the Cherry Compote:

- 1 cup (125 ml) water
- 1 cup (110 g) light brown sugar
- 2 cups (300 g) red cherries, pitted

For the Custard:

- 1 (15 fl. oz. or 420 ml) can sweetened condensed milk
- 1 cup (250 ml) milk
- 1 cup (250 g) heavy cream
- 2/3 cup (150 g) white sugar
- 8 whole eggs (about 60 g each)
- 1 teaspoon (5 ml) pure vanilla extract

METHOD

- Preheat and set your oven to 350 F (175 C).
- In a small non-stick saucepan, heat the water and sugar over medium heat. Shake and swirl occasionally to evenly distribute the sugar. Add the cherries and cook for 7 minutes. Remove from the heat source.
- In a large bowl, whisk together the sweetened condensed milk, milk, cream, eggs, and vanilla. Pour this mixture evenly into custard molds or ramekins and then cover with foil.
- Place the filled custard molds into a large baking dish and pour about an inch of hot water to the

baking dish. Bake in the preheated oven for about 45 minutes or until the custard is set. Let them cool at room temperature and then chill for at least 4 hours.

- Top with cherry compote before serving.
- Enjoy.

NUTRITIONAL INFORMATION

Energy	Fat	Carbohydrates	Protein	Sodium
311 calories	11.5 g	45.2 g	8.3 g	118 mg

BERRY CINNAMON CREME BRULEE

Preparation Time	Total Time	Yield
15 minutes	5 hours 15 minutes	6 servings

INGREDIENTS

- 8 egg yolks (about 20 g each)
- 6 tablespoons (90 g) white sugar, divided
- 1/2 teaspoon (2.5 ml) vanilla extract
- 2 1/2 cups (625 g) heavy cream
- 2 tablespoons (30 g) brown sugar
- 1 teaspoon (2 g) ground cinnamon
- Fresh raspberries, to serve
- Mint leaves, for garnish

METHOD

- Preheat and set your oven to 350 F (175 C).
- In a medium bowl, mix together the egg yolks, 4 tablespoons of white sugar, and vanilla extract until the mixture is thick and creamy. Set aside.
- Put the cream into a saucepan over low heat. Stir until it is almost boiling then remove from the heat source.
- Stir in egg yolk mixture and then pour the mixture into the top part of a double boiler. Fill the bottom part with water and bring to a simmer. Stir the cream mixture continuously for 3 minutes.
- Remove mixture from heat and pour into six ramekins.
- Bake for about 30-40 minutes then cool to room temperature. Chill for at least 4 hours.

- Combine remaining white sugar and brown sugar in a small bowl. Sprinkle on top of each custard. Using a kitchen blow torch, caramelize the sugar.
- To serve: Sprinkle with cinnamon, and then top with raspberries. Garnish with mint leaves.
- Serve and enjoy.

NUTRITIONAL INFORMATION

Energy	Fat	Carbohydrates	Protein	Sodium
180 calories	6.3 g	25.1 g	7.0 g	80 mg

MINI MERINGUE COOKIES

Preparation Time	Total Time	Yield
10 minutes	30 minutes	16 servings

INGREDIENTS

- 3 (40 g) egg whites
- 1 cup (220 g) white sugar
- 1/2 teaspoon (2 g) cream of tartar
- 1 teaspoon (5 ml) lemon juice

METHOD

- Preheat and set your oven to 300 F (150 C).
- Beat the egg whites in a metal bowl until foamy.
- Gradually, add sugar, cream of tartar, and lemon juice. Continue beating until stiff peaks form. To test if ready, simply lift your beater straight up, it should form stiff peaks.
- Spoon the meringue mixture into a piping bag fitted with star tip.
- Press the piping bag and drop a small star shaped meringue mixture onto a baking sheet. Repeat with remaining mixture.
- Bake in the preheated oven for 20-25 minutes or until golden and dry on the outside. Let them cool at room temperature.
- Transfer to a serving dish.
- Serve and enjoy.

NUTRITIONAL INFORMATION

Energy	Fat	Carbohydrates	Protein	Sodium
51 calories	0.0 g	12.6 g	0.8 g	8 mg

EGG SALAD ON TOASTS

Preparation Time	Total Time	Yield
10 minutes	30 minutes	12 servings

INGREDIENTS

- 5 hard-boiled eggs, chopped
- 1 (40 g) shallot, minced
- 3/4 cup (180 g) light mayonnaise
- 1 tablespoon (15 g) Dijon mustard
- 1 tablespoon (15 ml) lemon juice
- 2 tablespoons (7 g) fresh parsley, chopped
- 1 baguette (250 g), cut into 12 slices crosswise
- Salt and freshly ground black pepper

METHOD

- In a medium bowl, combine the chopped eggs, shallot, mayonnaise, Dijon mustard, lemon juice, and parsley. Season to taste.
- Place the bread slices into the toaster then toast until golden brown.
- Equally divide the egg salad mixture and spread evenly onto each toast.
- Serve and enjoy.

NUTRITIONAL INFORMATION

Energy	Fat	Carbohydrates	Protein	Sodium
162 calories	7.4 g	18.3 g	6.0 g	423 mg

EGG ON AVOCADO BOAT

Preparation Time	Total Time	Yield
10 minutes	30 minutes	4 servings

INGREDIENTS

- 2 ripe avocados (about 200 g each), pitted and halved lengthwise
- 4 large eggs (about 60 g each)
- 3 (1 oz. or 30g) slices of turkey bacon
- Chopped fresh parsley, for garnish
- Salt and freshly ground black pepper

METHOD

- Preheat and set your oven to 350 F (175 C).
- Place the avocado halves in a baking dish, then crack 1 egg onto each hollow part of the avocado. Season to taste.
- Bake until the egg whites are set, and yolks are no longer runny, about 15 minutes
- Meanwhile, in a large pan over a moderate flame, cook the turkey bacon until crisp, about 7 minutes.
- Drain the oil by transferring to a plate lined with paper towels.
- Chop the bacon slices then place on top of avocados. Sprinkle with chopped parsley.
- Serve and enjoy.

NUTRITIONAL INFORMATION

Energy	Fat	Carbohydrates	Protein	Sodium
304 calories	25.3 g	9.0 g	12.3 g	434 mg

SPICED DEVILLED EGGS

Preparation Time	Total Time	Yield
15 minutes	15 minutes	12 servings

INGREDIENTS

- 6 (60 g) hard-boiled eggs
- 3/4 cup (185 g) mayonnaise
- 2 tablespoons (30 g) Dijon mustard
- 1 tablespoon (15 g) pickle relish
- 1/2 teaspoon (1 g) wholegrain mustard
- 1/2 teaspoon (1 g) cumin, ground
- 1/2 teaspoon (1 g) cayenne pepper
- 1/2 teaspoon (1 g) coriander seed, ground
- Salt and freshly ground black pepper
- Paprika, to serve
- Fresh chives, for garnish

METHOD

- Remove and discard the shells from the eggs. Cut them in half lengthwise.
- With a spoon, scoop out the egg yolks, and then put them in a medium bowl.
- Add the mayonnaise, Dijon mustard, pickle relish, cumin, cayenne, and coriander. Season to taste. Mix well. Transfer the egg mixture into a piping bag fitted with a star tip.
- Pipe the egg mixture onto the hollow part of the egg white halves. Sprinkle with paprika and garnish with fresh chives.
- Serve and enjoy.

NUTRITIONAL INFORMATION

Energy	Fat	Carbohydrates	Protein	Sodium
109 calories	9.2 g	5.5 g	3.8 g	270 mg

RECIPE INDEX

Z

Made in the USA
Las Vegas, NV
17 February 2024

85932634R00075